ARTIST DESCENDING A STAIRCASE

ARTIST
DESCENDING
A STAIRCASE

TOM STOPPARD

faber and faber
LONDON · BOSTON

First published in 1973
with *Where Are They Now?*
by Faber and Faber Limited
3 Queen Square London WC1N 3AU
Reprinted 1976 and 1979
Reissued as a single volume in 1988
Printed in Great Britain by
Richard Clay Ltd, Bungay, Suffolk
All rights reserved

Quality Printing and Binding by:
R.R. Donnelly & Sons Company
1009 Sloan Street
Crawfordsville, IN 47933 U.S.A.

To my Mother and Father

Author's Note

Artist Descending a Staircase was written for radio and is here reissued in its original form. However, it seems to have turned itself into a stage play meanwhile. Several times since the broadcast in 1972 I had been asked to permit a stage production, but I was never very keen on the idea. My argument was that if I had written it for the stage I would have written it differently; and my conceit was that in writing the play for radio I had tried to use the medium in such a way as to make *Artist Descending a Staircase* a 'radio play' of necessity. I trusted that a stage version would merely prove that I had succeeded in this. In the event, the King's Head Theatre proved to most people's satisfaction, including my own, that I had failed. For this I must thank the impresario Dan Crawford, the director Tim Luscombe, and the excellent King's Head Company.

The adaptation required virtually no changes in the dialogue. There are three settings: the elderly artists' studio; the young artists' drawing room in Lambeth; and open country somewhere on the border of France and Germany. For obvious reasons the published text mentions only sound effects. These basic stage directions at the top of the scenes may help to visualize the play:

SCENE ONE

Two elderly artists, MARTELLO *and* BEAUCHAMP, *are standing quietly listening to a tape-recorder. The machine is not up to date, even for the 1970s, being something of a museum piece. The room is evidently a studio shared, as it turns out, by three artists. It is a large attic space, approached from below by a staircase which disappears out of view. The top of the staircase is protected by a wooden balustrade. The balustrade is now broken. The attic contains various tools of the trade, including a canvas on an easel and a life-size female figure, suggesting a piece of early surrealism, whose details will emerge from the dialogue. In general, the room conforms to what the play tells us, that three artists have lived and worked here for many years and not always harmoniously.*

The machine is playing and replaying a loop of tape. Evidently BEAUCHAMP *has adapted his machine so that it records and re-records, without wiping, on the same loop. Such a machine would certainly not be capable of this trick without a good deal of ingenuity on* BEAU-CHAMP's *part so it would be as well if the apparatus indicated this.*

SCENE TWO

The attic studio. The balustrade is now unbroken. DON-NER *is working at the easel. He is painting* 'A naked woman sitting about a garden with a unicorn eating the roses'. BEAUCHAMP *is busy with his own art form: listening appreciatively to his latest tape, which is a tonal collage of random noises, sighs, squeaks, human and mechanical, randomly captured and layered over each other, interspersed by periods of relative quiet.* BEAU-CHAMP *allows the tape to play for a while and then turns it off.*

SCENE THREE

DONNER *has brought* MARTELLO *a cup of tea, and one for himself.* MARTELLO *has paused in working on his surreal female figure.* DONNER *has paused in working on his 'edible art'—perhaps carving a block of salt.* MARTELLO *has borrowed* DONNER's *newest work, a sugar Venus de Milo, and is scraping her into his cup of tea.*

SCENE FOUR

An upper room in Lambeth, introduced by distant music from an accordion, clichéd Parisian music. YOUNG BEAUCHAMP, *who is in his mid-twenties, is shutting and strapping up a leather suitcase.* SOPHIE, *aged twenty-two, stands facing a window which is high up in the building. They are dressed for the street.*

SCENE FIVE

The Lambeth room, now containing, in addition, all the personal belongings of the three young men who share it as a drawing room. These objects include a wind-up gramophone, which is now playing a record but the sounds are only of a ping-pong game in progress. YOUNG DONNER *and* YOUNG BEAUCHAMP *are present and* MARTELLO *can be heard approaching from downstairs, with* SOPHIE.

SCENE SIX

Countryside with woods. The three young artists are on a walking holiday on the Continent. They are furnished with knapsacks, walking sticks, and so forth. BEAUCHAMP, *in addition, is making hoof-beat noises with the two halves of a coconut shell.* MARTELLO *has a map.*

SCENE SEVEN

The Lambeth drawing room. The tea party continues. Everyone in high spirits. SOPHIE *is moving about the room, one pace at a time, directed by the enthusiastic instructions of her hosts.*

SCENE EIGHT

The empty Lambeth room, with faint accordion music. DONNER *stands quietly listening to* SOPHIE.

SCENE NINE

The attic room. OLD MARTELLO *and* OLD DONNER *have resumed their labours of art. The balustrade is unbroken.*

SCENE TEN

The attic room. DONNER *is working at his painting.* BEAUCHAMP *is working with his tape-recorder but has paused to try to kill the elusive fly. He thumps the table. The balustrade is unbroken.*

SCENE ELEVEN

The attic room. The balustrade is now broken. BEAU-CHAMP *and* MARTELLO *listening to the original loop of tape. They listen to the sound of* DONNER *falling down the stairs.*

Artist Descending a Staircase received its first production on BBC Radio 3 on 14 November, 1972. The cast was as follows:

MARTELLO (SENIOR)	Stephen Murray
BEAUCHAMP (SENIOR)	Rolf Lefebvre
DONNER (SENIOR)	Carleton Hobbs
SOPHIE	Fiona Walker
MARTELLO (JUNIOR)	Michael Spice
BEAUCHAMP (JUNIOR)	Peter Egan
DONNER (JUNIOR)	Dinsdale Landen

Produced by John Tydeman

The play was first performed on stage at the King's Head Theatre, Islington, from 2 August to 10 September 1988. The cast was as follows:

MARTELLO (SENIOR)	William Lucas
MARTELLO (JUNIOR)	Karl James
BEAUCHAMP (SENIOR)	Peter Copley
BEAUCHAMP (JUNIOR)	Gareth Tudor Price
DONNER (SENIOR)	Frank Midlemass
DONNER (JUNIOR)	John Warnaby
SOPHIE	Sarah Woodward

Director	Tim Luscombe
Decor	Martin Chitty
Costumes	Tim Heywood
Sound	Kevin Malpass

This production transferred to the Duke of York's Theatre, London, on 7 December 1988, where the part of DONNER SENIOR was played by Alan Macnaughton.

Note

There are eleven scenes. The play begins in the here-and-now; the next five scenes are each a flash-back from the previous scene; the seventh, eighth, ninth, tenth and eleventh scenes are, respectively, continuations of the fifth, fourth, third, second and first. So the play is set temporally in six parts, in the sequence ABCDEFEDCBA.

A = here and now
B = a couple of hours ago
C = Last week
D = 1922
E = 1920
F = 1914

We hear, on a continuous loop of tape, a sequence of sounds which is to be interpreted by MARTELLO *and* BEAUCHAMP *thus:*

(a) DONNER *dozing: an irregular droning noise.*

(b) *Careful footsteps approach. The effect is stealthy. A board creaks.*

(c) *This wakes* DONNER, *i.e., the droning stops in mid-beat.*

(d) *The footsteps freeze.*

(e) DONNER's *voice, unalarmed: 'Ah! There you are . . .'*

(f) *Two more quick steps, and then Thump!*

(f) DONNER *cries out.*

(h) *Wood cracks as he falls through a balustrade.*

(i) *He falls heavily down the stairs, with a final sickening thump when he hits the bottom. Silence.*

After a pause, this entire sequence begins again . . . Droning . . . Footsteps . . . (as before).

MARTELLO: I think this is where I came in.

1

(TAPE: *'Ah! There you are . . .'*)

BEAUCHAMP: And this is where you hit him.

(TAPE: *Thump!)*

MARTELLO: I *mean,* it's going round again. The tape is going round in a *loop.*

BEAUCHAMP: Well, of course. I record in loops, lassoing my material—no, like trawling— no, like—no matter.

(TAPE: DONNER *reaches the bottom of the stairs.)*

MARTELLO: Poor Donner.

(MARTELLO *and* BEAUCHAMP *are old men, as was* DONNER.
(The TAPE *starts off again as before.)*

BEAUCHAMP *(over* TAPE): Round and round, re- cording layer upon layer of silence while Donner dozed after a heavy lunch, the spools quietly folding silence upon itself, yes like packing linen into trunks . . . Fold, fold until the footsteps broke it . . . and woke him——

2

(TAPE: *'Ah! There you are . . .'*)

How peaceful it was, in the afternoon in the great houses before the Great War, to doze after luncheon with only a fly buzzing in the stuffy room and a sense of the maids somewhere quietly folding the linen into pine chests . . .

(TAPE: DONNER *reaches the bottom of the stairs.*)

Donner knew the post-prandial nap. His people were excellently connected. With mine, in fact.

(TAPE: *re-continues under.*)

I suppose we should let someone know, though not necessarily the entire circumstances. I'm not one to tell tales if no good can come of it.

MARTELLO: I will stand by you, Beauchamp. We have been together a long time.

BEAUCHAMP: You may rely on me, Martello. I shall not cast the first stone.

MARTELLO: You *have* cast it, Beauchamp, but I do not prejudge you.

BEAUCHAMP: My feelings precisely, but there seems to be some confusion in your mind——

MARTELLO: My very thought. Turn off your machine, it seems to be disturbing your concentration——

(TAPE: *'Ah!——' and is switched off.*)

BEAUCHAMP: There you are.

MARTELLO: On the contrary, Beauchamp, there *you* are. Unless we can agree on *that*, I can't even begin to help you clear up this mess.

BEAUCHAMP: Don't touch him, Martello.

MARTELLO: I don't mean clear up *Donner!*— honestly, Beauchamp, you buffoon!

BEAUCHAMP: Cynic!

MARTELLO: Geriatric!

BEAUCHAMP: Murderer!

4

(Pause.)

MARTELLO: As I was saying, I shall help you so far as I can to get through the difficult days ahead, whether in duplicity or in the police courts, depending on how you intend to face the situation; but I shall do so only on the condition that we drop this farce of accusation and counter-accusation. You had only two friends in the world, and having killed one you can't afford to irritate the other.

BEAUCHAMP: Very well!—I gave you your chance, and now I'm going to get the police.

MARTELLO: A very sensible decision. You are too feeble to run, and too forgetful to tell lies consistent with each other. Furthermore, you are too old to make the gain worth the trouble. Be absolutely frank with them, but do not plead insanity. That would reflect undeserved credit on three generations of art critics.

BEAUCHAMP: I must say, Martello, I have to admire your gall.

MARTELLO: Stress all mitigating factors, such as Donner's refusal to clean the bath after use, and his infuriating mannerisms any of which might have got him murdered years ago. Remember how John used to say, 'If Donner whistles the opening of Beethoven's Fifth in six/eight time once more I'll *kill him!*'?

BEAUCHAMP: John who?

MARTELLO: Augustus John.

BEAUCHAMP: No, no, it was Edith Sitwell.

MARTELLO: Rubbish!—you're getting old, Beauchamp.

BEAUCHAMP: I am two years younger than you, Martello.

MARTELLO: Anybody who is two years younger than me is *senile*. It is only by a great effort of will that my body has not decomposed. Which reminds me, you can't leave Donner lying there at the bottom of the stairs for very long in this weather, and that is only the practical argument; how long can you *ethically* leave him?

BEAUCHAMP: It is nothing to do with me.

MARTELLO: Beauchamp, I am shocked. You were at school together. You signed his first manifesto, as he signed yours. You have conjured with his name and travelled on his ticket; shared his roof, his prejudices, his occasional grant; eaten his bread and drunk his health (God forgive my *brain!*—it is so attuned to the ironic tone it has become ironical in repose; I have to whip sincerity out of it as one whips responses from a mule!)—to put it plain, you have been friends for over sixty years.

BEAUCHAMP: Well, the same goes for you.

MARTELLO: Yes, but you killed him.

BEAUCHAMP: I did no such thing!, and you have good reason to know it! I am thoroughly disillusioned in you, Martello. I was willing to bend over backwards to see your side of it, but I can't stand a chap who won't come clean when he's found out.

MARTELLO: I, on the other hand, admire your hopeless persistence. But the tape recorder speaks for itself. That is, of course, the point about tape recorders. In this case it is eloquent, grandiloquent, not to say Grundigloquent—Oh God, if only I could turn it *off!*—

7

no wonder I have achieved nothing with my life!—my brain is on a flying trapeze that outstrips all the possibilities of action. Mental acrobatics, Beauchamp—I have achieved nothing but mental acrobatics—*nothing!*—whereas you, however wrongly and for whatever reason, came to grips with life at least this once, and killed Donner.

BEAUCHAMP: It's not true, Martello!

MARTELLO: Yes, yes, I tell you, *nothing!*— Niente! Nada! Nichts!—Oh, a few pieces here and there, a few scandals—Zurich— Paris—Buenos Aires—but, all in all, nothing, not even among the nihilists! *(Pause.)* I tell you, Beauchamp, it's no secret between us that I never saw much point in your tonal art. I remember saying to Sophie, in the early days when you were still using gramophone discs, Beauchamp is wasting his time, I said, there'll be no revelations coming out of *that;* no truth. And the critics won't listen either. And they didn't. But this time you've got them by the ears. It has the impact of newsreel. In my opinion it's a *tour de force.*

BEAUCHAMP: You are clearly deranged. It is probably the first time a murderer has tried to justify himself on artistic grounds. As it happens, you are also misguided. Far from creating a *tour de force*, you ruined what would have been a strand in my master-work of accumulated silence, and left in its place a melodramatic fragment whose point will not be lost on a jury.

(He presses TAPE *switch: '—There you are ——' etc.)*

There indeed he is, ladies and gentlemen, caught by the fortuitous presence of a recording machine that had been left running in the room where Mr. Donner was quietly working on a portrait from memory, a portrait fated to be unfinished.

MARTELLO: Poor Donner, he never had much luck with Sophie.

BEAUCHAMP: For the existence of this recording we have to thank Mr. Beauchamp, a fact which argues his innocence, where it ever in doubt. Mr. Beauchamp, an artist who may be familiar to some of you——

MARTELLO: If you are extremely old and collect trivia——

9

BEAUCHAMP: —and his friends, Mr. Donner and the man Martello, lived and worked together in a single large attic studio approached by a staircase, which led upwards from the landing, and was guarded at the top by an insubstantial rail, through which, as you will hear, Mr. Donner fell.

MARTELLO: An accident, really.

BEAUCHAMP: If you say so.

MARTELLO: You didn't mean to *kill* him. It was manslaughter.

BEAUCHAMP: You will hear how Mr. Donner, while working, dozed off in his chair . . .

(TAPE: *Droning.*)

Footsteps approach.

(TAPE: *Footsteps.*)

Someone has entered quietly. Who? No visitors came to this place. Martello and Mr. Beauchamp met their acquaintances outside, formerly at the Savage, lattery in public houses. And Mr. Donner, who was somewhat reclusive, not to say misanthropic, had no friends at all—except the other two, *a fact whose importance speaks for itself*——

(TAPE: *'Ah! There you are . . .'—and is switched off.*)

Not, 'Who the devil are you?', or 'Good Lord, what are you doing here, I haven't seen you for donkey's years!'—no. 'Ah, there you are.' The footsteps can only have belonged to the man Martello.

MARTELLO: Or, of course, the man Beauchamp. I don't see where this is getting us—we already know perfectly well that it was *one* of us, and it is absurd that you should prevaricate in this way when there is no third party to impress. I came home to find Donner dead, and you at the top of the stairs, fiddling with your tape-recorder. It is quite clear that I arrived just in time to stop you wiping out the evidence.

BEAUCHAMP: But it was *I* who came home and found Donner dead—with your footsteps on the machine. My first thought was to preserve any evidence it had picked up, so I very quietly ascended——

11

MARTELLO: Beauchamp, why are you bothering to lie to *me?* You are like a man on a desert island refusing to admit to his only companion that he ate the last coconut.

BEAUCHAMP: For the very good reason that while my back was turned you shinned up the tree and guzzled it. And *incidentally*—I see that you have discovered where I keep my special marmalade. That's *stealing,* Martello, common theft. That marmalade does *not* come out of the housekeeping——

MARTELLO: It must have been Donner.

BEAUCHAMP: It was not Donner. Donner never cleaned the tub and he always helped himself to cheese in such a way as to leave all the rind, but he never stole my marmalade because he didn't *like* marmalade. He did steal my *honey,* I know that for a fact. And he had the nerve to accuse me of taking the top off the milk.

MARTELLO: Well, you do.

BEAUCHAMP *(furiously):* Because I have paid the milkman four weeks running! It's *my milk!*

MARTELLO: I suppose we should leave a note for him. Two pints a day will be enough now.

BEAUCHAMP: Since you will be in jail, one pint will be ample. Poor Donner. He was not so easy to get on with in recent years, but I shall always regret that my last conversation with him was not more friendly.

MARTELLO: Were you rowing about the housekeeping again?

BEAUCHAMP: No, no. He was rather unfeeling about my work in progress, as a matter of fact.

MARTELLO: He was rude about mine the other day. He attacked it.

BEAUCHAMP: He said mine was rubbish.

MARTELLO: Did he attack you? Was that it?

BEAUCHAMP: Why did he resent me? He seemed embittered, lately . . .

MARTELLO: He'd been brooding about Sophie.

13

BEAUCHAMP: And that ridiculous painting. What was the matter with the man?

MARTELLO: I think I was rather at fault . . .

BEAUCHAMP: I paid him the compliment of letting him hear how my master-tape was progressing . . .

Flashback

(BEAUCHAMP*'s 'master-tape' is a bubbling cauldron of squeaks, gurgles, crackles, and other unharmonious noises. He allows it to play for longer than one would reasonably hope.*)

BEAUCHAMP: Well, what do you think of it, Donner? Take your time, choose your words carefully.

DONNER: I think it's rubbish.

BEAUCHAMP: Oh. You mean, a sort of tonal debris, as it were?

DONNER: No, rubbish, general rubbish. In the sense of being worthless, without value; rot, nonsense. Rubbish, in fact.

BEAUCHAMP: Ah. The detritus of audible existence, a sort of refuse heap of sound . . .

DONNER: I mean, *rubbish*. I'm sorry, Beauchamp, but you must come to terms with the fact that our paths have diverged. I very much enjoyed my years in that child's garden of easy victories known as the avant garde, but I am now engaged in the infinitely more difficult task of painting what the eye sees.

BEAUCHAMP: Well, I've never seen a naked woman sitting about a garden with a unicorn eating the roses.

DONNER: Don't split hairs with *me*, Beauchamp. You don't know what art is. Those tape recordings of yours are the mechanical expression of a small intellectual idea, the kind of notion that might occur to a man in his bath and be forgotten in the business of drying between his toes. You can call it art if you like, but it is the commonplace of any ironic imagination, and there are thousands of clerks and shop assistants who would be astonished to be called artists on their bath night.

BEAUCHAMP: Wait a minute, Donner——

DONNER: And they, incidentally, would call your tapes——

BEAUCHAMP: Quiet!——

DONNER: —rubbish.

(Smack!)

BEAUCHAMP: Missed him! I don't want that fly buzzing around the microphone—I'm starting up a new loop.

DONNER: I see I'm wasting my breath.

BEAUCHAMP: I heard you. Clerks—bath-night —rubbish, and so on. But my tapes are not for clerks. They are for initiates, as is all art.

DONNER: My kind is for Everyman.

BEAUCHAMP: Only because every man is an initiate of that particular mystery. But your painting is not for dogs, parrots, bicycles . . . You select your public. It is the same with me, but my tapes have greater mystery —they elude dogs, parrots, clerks and the greater part of mankind. If you played my tape on the radio, it would seem a meaningless noise, because it fulfils no expectations:

16

people have been taught to expect certain kinds of insight but not others. The first duty of the artist is to capture the radio station.

DONNER: It was Lewis who said that.

BEAUCHAMP: Lewis who?

DONNER: Wyndham Lewis.

BEAUCHAMP: It was Edith Sitwell, as a matter of fact.

DONNER: Rubbish.

BEAUCHAMP: She came out with it while we were dancing.

DONNER: You never danced with Edith Sitwell.

BEAUCHAMP: Oh yes I did.

DONNER: You're thinking of that American woman who sang negro spirituals at Nancy Cunard's coming-out ball.

BEAUCHAMP: It was Queen Mary's wedding, as a matter of fact.

DONNER: You're mad.

BEAUCHAMP: I don't mean wedding, I mean launching.

DONNER: I can understand your confusion but it was Nancy Cunard's coming-out.

BEAUCHAMP: Down at the docks?

DONNER: British boats are not launched to the sound of minstrel favourites.

BEAUCHAMP: I don't mean launching, I mean maiden voyage.

DONNER: I refuse to discuss it. Horrible noise, anyway.

BEAUCHAMP: Only because people have not been taught what to listen for, or how to listen.

DONNER: What are you talking about?

BEAUCHAMP: Really, Donner, your mind keeps wandering about in a senile chaos! My *tape*. If I had one good man placed high up in the BBC my tape would become art for millions, in time.

DONNER: It would not become art. It would become a mildly interesting noise instead of a totally meaningless noise. An artist is someone who is gifted in some way which enables him to do something more or less well which can only be done badly or not at all by someone who is not thus gifted. To speak of an art which requires no gift is a contradiction employed by people like yourself who have an artistic bent but no particular skill.

(Smack!)

BEAUCHAMP: Missed!

DONNER: An artistic imagination coupled with skill is talent.

BEAUCHAMP: Where is he?—Ah——

(Smack!)

Damn!

DONNER: Skill without imagination is craftsmanship and gives us many useful objects such as wickerwork picnic baskets. Imagination without skill gives us modern art.

BEAUCHAMP: A perfectly reasonable summary.

(Thump!, fist on desk.)

DONNER: Beauchamp!

BEAUCHAMP: Did you get him?

DONNER: I am trying to open your eyes to the nakedness of your emperor.

BEAUCHAMP: But Donner, ever since I've known you you've been running around asking for the name of his tailor—symbolism, surrealism, imagism, vorticism, fauvism, cubism—dada, drip-action, hard-edge, pop, found objects and post-object—it's only a matter of days since you spent the entire housekeeping on sugar to make an edible Venus de Milo, and now you've discovered the fashions of your childhood. What *happened* to you?

DONNER: I have returned to traditional values, that is where the true history of art continues to lie, not in your small jokes. I make no apology for the past, but precocity at our age is faintly ludicrous, don't you think?

BEAUCHAMP: At our age, *any*thing we do is faintly ludicrous. Our best hope as artists is to transcend our limitations and become *ut-*

terly ludicrous. Which you are proceeding to do with your portrait of Sophie, for surely you can see that a post-Pop pre-Raphaelite is pure dada brought up to date——

(Smack!)

DONNER: Shut up, damn you!—how dare you talk of her?!—how dare you——

(And weeps——)

—and would you stop cleaning the bath with my face flannel!!! (Pause.) I'm sorry— please accept my apology——

BEAUCHAMP: I'm sorry, Donner . . . I had no idea you felt so strongly about it.

DONNER: *(Sniffle.)* Well, I have to wash my face with it.

BEAUCHAMP: No, no, I mean about your new . . . Donner, what *has* happened?—What happened between you and Martello? You have not been yourself . . . since you smashed your Venus and began your portrait . . . You have . . . shunned me——

DONNER: I did not intend to.

BEAUCHAMP: Have I offended you? Is it about the milk?

DONNER: No. I have just been—sad.

BEAUCHAMP: Do you blame me for Sophie?

DONNER: I don't know. It was a long time ago now. It *is* becoming a good likeness, isn't it?

BEAUCHAMP: Oh yes. She would have liked it. I mean if she could have seen it. A real Academy picture . . . !

DONNER: Yes.

BEAUCHAMP: I don't know, Donner . . . before the war, in Soho, you were always making plans to smuggle a live ostrich into the Royal Academy; and now look at you. In Zurich in 1915 you told Tarzan he was too conservative.

DONNER: Tarzan?

BEAUCHAMP: I don't mean Tarzan. Who do I mean? Similar name, conservative, 1915 . . .

DONNER: Tsar Nicholas?

BEAUCHAMP: No, no, Zurich.

DONNER: I remember Zurich . . . after our walking tour. God, what a walk! You were crazy Beauchamp, you and your horse.

BEAUCHAMP: I'll never forget it. That really was a walk. When we got to Zurich, my boots were worn to paper. Sat in the Café Rousseau and put my feet up, ordered a lemon squash.

DONNER: The Café Rousseau was Monte Carlo later.

BEAUCHAMP: Monte Carlo was the Café Russe.

DONNER: Was it?

BEAUCHAMP: Put my feet up and ordered a citron pressé in the Café Rousseau.

DONNER: Still doesn't sound right.

BEAUCHAMP: Couldn't have it—no lemons. The waiter was very apologetic. No lemons because of the war, he said. Good God, I said, is Switzerland at war?—things have come to a pretty pass, is it the St. Bernard? —Not a smile. Man at the next table laughed out loud and offered me a glass of squash made from lemon powder, remarking, 'If lemons don't exist, it is necessary to invent them.' It seemed wittier at the time, I don't know why.

DONNER: Voltaire!—of course, the Café Voltaire!

BEAUCHAMP: That was a rum bird.

DONNER: Voltaire?

BEAUCHAMP: No, Lenin.

DONNER: Oh yes. Very rum.

BEAUCHAMP: Very liberal with his lemon powder but a rum bird nevertheless. Edith saw through him right away. She said to him, 'I don't know what you're waiting for but it's not going to happen in Switzerland.' Of course, she was absolutely right.

DONNER: Edith was never in Switzerland. Your memory is playing you up again.

BEAUCHAMP: Oh yes she was.

DONNER: Not that time. That time was Hugo Ball and Hans Arp Max, Kurt, André . . . Picabia . . . Tristan Tzara——

BEAUCHAMP: That was him!

DONNER: What was?

BEAUCHAMP: Conservative. But he had audacity. Wrote his name in the snow, and said, 'There! . . . I think I'll call it The Alps.'

DONNER: That was Marcel. He used to beat Lenin at chess. I think he had talent under all those jokes. He said to me, 'There are two ways of becoming an artist. The first way is to do the things by which is meant art. The second way is to make art mean the things you do.' What a stroke of genius! It made anything possible and everything safe!— safe from criticism, since our art admitted no standards outside itself; safe from comparison, since it had no history; safe from evaluation, since it referred to no system of values beyond the currency it had invented. We were no longer accountable. We were artists by mutual agreement.

BEAUCHAMP: So was everyone from Praxiteles to Rodin. There's nothing divine about classical standards; it's just a bigger club.

DONNER: It seems there is something divine about modern art nonetheless, for it is only sustained by faith. That is why artists have become as complacent as priests. They do not have to demonstrate their truths. Like priests they demand our faith that something is more than it appears to be—bread, wine, a tin of soup, a twisted girder, a mauve square, a meaningless collection of sounds on a loop of tape . . .

(This is said so bitterly that——)

BEAUCHAMP: Donner . . . what happened?—what did Martello say to you?

DONNER: It really doesn't matter. And how do I know he wasn't lying, just getting his own back?—you see, I damaged his figure, slightly . . . He was working on it—I didn't know what it was—And I brought him a cup of tea——

Flashback

(MARTELLO *is scraping and chipping, and clicking his tongue, and scraping again. He sighs.)*

DONNER: That's it—help yourself to sugar.

MARTELLO: I'm not getting any. She's set too hard.

DONNER: Knock off one of her nipples.

MARTELLO: I'd need a chisel.

DONNER: Wait a minute. I'll tilt her over. Get the breast into your cup, and I'll stir her around a bit.

MARTELLO: What a ridiculous business. How am I going to sprinkle her on my cornflakes?

DONNER: Starving peasants don't have cornflakes. Good God, Martello, if they had any corn do you think they'd turn it into a sunshine breakfast for figure-conscious typists?

MARTELLO: What the hell are you talking about? What starving peasants? Honestly, Donner, you go from one extreme to the other. On the whole I preferred your ceramic sugar lumps.

DONNER: No, I got the whole thing back to front with my ceramic food. Of course, ceramic bread and steak and strawberries with plaster-of-paris cream defined the problem very neatly, but I was still avoiding the answer. The question remained: how can one justify a work of art to a man with an empty belly? The answer, like all great insights, was simple: make it edible.

MARTELLO: Brilliant.

DONNER: It came to me in my—incidentally, is it you who keeps using my face-cloth to clean the tub?

MARTELLO: No. It must be Beauchamp.

DONNER: That man has absolutely no respect for property.

MARTELLO: I know. And he's taken to hiding the marmalade. Do you happen to know where it is?

DONNER: In the pickle jar.

MARTELLO: Cunning devil! Thank you.

DONNER: The olive oil is really honey.

MARTELLO: Incredible. It probably came to him in his bath, while he was using your flannel.

DONNER: Where is he?

MARTELLO: He went out to get some more sugar, out of his own money. I wonder where he'll hide it.

DONNER: Let him. Sugar art is only the beginning.

MARTELLO: It will give cubism a new lease on life.

DONNER: Think of Le Penseur sculpted in . . .

MARTELLO: Cold rice pudding.

DONNER: Salt. Think of poor villages getting a month's supply of salt in the form of classical sculpture!

MARTELLO: And not just classical!—your own pieces, reproduced indelibly yet edibly——

DONNER: Think of pizza pies raised to the level of Van Gogh sunflowers!—think of a whole new range of pigments, from salt to liquorice!

MARTELLO: Your signed loaves of bread reproduced in sculpted dough, *baked* . . . your ceramic steaks carved from meat! It will give opinion back to the intellectuals and put taste where it belongs. From now on the artist's palate——

DONNER: Are you laughing at me, Martello?

MARTELLO: Certainly not, Donner. Let them eat art.

DONNER: Imagine my next exhibition, thrown open to the hungry . . . You know, Martello, for the first time I feel free of that small sense of shame which every artist lives with. I think, in a way, edible art is what we've all been looking for.

MARTELLO: Who?

DONNER: All of us!—Breton!—Ernst!—Marcel —Max—you—me—Remember how Pablo used to shout that the war had made art irrelevant?—well——

MARTELLO: Which Pablo?

DONNER: What do you mean, which Pablo?— *Pablo!*

MARTELLO: What, that one-armed waiter at the Café Suisse?

DONNER: Yes—the Café Russe—the proprietor, lost a leg at Verdun——

MARTELLO: God, he was slow, that Pablo. But it's amazing how you remember all the people who gave you credit . . .

DONNER: He gave you credit because you had been at Verdun.

MARTELLO: That's true.

DONNER: It was a lie.

MARTELLO: Wasn't I? It must have been pretty close to Verdun, our route was right through that bit of country, remember it well.

DONNER: God yes, what a walk. You were crazy, Martello.

MARTELLO: I must have been, I suppose.

DONNER: Beauchamp was crazy too.

MARTELLO: Him and his horse.

DONNER: That was about the last really good time we had . . .

MARTELLO: You hated it.

DONNER: No.

MARTELLO: More than the war.

DONNER: That's what killed it for me. After that, being an artist made no sense. I should have stopped then. Art made no sense.

MARTELLO: Except for nonsense art. Pablo never understood the difference. He used to get so angry about his missing arm——

DONNER: (leg . . .)

MARTELLO: I can see him now—a tray in each hand, swearing . . . wait a minute——

DONNER: *Leg.*

MARTELLO: A tray in each leg—Are you deliberately trying to confuse me?

DONNER: He was right. He understood exactly. There *wasn't* any difference. We tried to make a distinction between the art that celebrated reason and history and logic and all assumptions, and our own dislocated anti-art of lost faith—but it was all the same insult to a one-legged soldier and the one-legged, one-armed, one-eyed regiment of the maimed. And here we are still at it, looking for another twist. Finally the only thing I can say in defence of my figure is that you can eat it.

MARTELLO: And of mine that you can smile at it. How do you like her?

DONNER: It looks like a scarecrow trying to be a tailor's dummy. Is it symbolic?

MARTELLO: Metaphorical.

DONNER: Why has she got straw on her head?

MARTELLO: Not straw—ripe corn. It's her hair. It was either ripe corn or spun gold, and I wouldn't know how to do that, it was bad enough getting the pearls for her teeth.

DONNER: They look like false teeth.

MARTELLO: Well of course they're artificial pearls. So are the rubies, of course. I know you'll appreciate her breasts.

DONNER: Oh yes. Are they edible?

MARTELLO: Well, you're not supposed to eat them—I'm only using real fruit for the moment, and real feathers for her swan-like neck. I don't know how to do her eyes: stars seem somehow inappropriate . . . Would you have described them as dark pools, perhaps?

DONNER: Who?

MARTELLO: Well, Sophie of course.

DONNER: Are you telling me that that *thing* is supposed to be Sophie?

MARTELLO: Metaphorically.

DONNER: You cad, Martello!

MARTELLO: I beg your pardon?

DONNER: You unspeakable rotter! Is nothing sacred to you?

MARTELLO: Hold on, Donner, no offence intended.

DONNER: What right have you to sneer at her memory?—I won't allow it, damn you! My

God, she had a sad enough life without having her beauty mocked in death by your
contemptible artistic presumptions——

(Thump! A pearl bounces . . .)

MARTELLO: Now steady on, Donner, you've
knocked out one of her teeth.

DONNER *(by now nearly weeping):* Oh Sophie
. . . I cannot think of beauty without re-
membering your innocent grace, your hair
like . . .

MARTELLO: Ripe corn——

DONNER: Gold. Your tragic gaze—eyes like——

MARTELLO: Stars——

DONNER: Bottomless pools, and when you
laughed——

MARTELLO: Teeth like pearls——

DONNER: It was like a silver bell whose sound
parted your pale ruby lips——

MARTELLO: *A silver bell!*—yes!—behind her
breasts——

DONNER: —were like——

MARTELLO: —ripe pears——

DONNER: Firm young apples——

MARTELLO: Pears—For heaven's sake control yourself, Donner, those are real artificial pearls——

(Pearls bouncing—DONNER thumping, gasping . . .)

DONNER: Oh Sophie . . . I try to shut out the memory but it needs only . . . a ribbon . . . a flower . . . a phrase of music . . . a river flowing beneath ancient bridges . . . the scent of summertime . . .

(Cliché Paris music, accordion . . .)

Flashback

(Keep music in. Fade.)

SOPHIE: I must say I won't be entirely sorry to leave Lambeth—the river smells like a dead cat, and the accordionist downstairs is driving me insane . . .

(SOPHIE *is 22 and not at all bitter. Background is sound of leather suitcase being snapped shut and strapped up by* YOUNG BEAUCHAMP *who is in his mid-20s.*)

If only someone would give him a job, elsewhere, even for a few minutes. Or perhaps we could employ him to take down our suitcases. He'd have to put his accordion down for that. But then he'd probably whistle through his teeth. I'm sorry to be so useless, darling . . . Are the others downstairs? . . . Yes . . . that's them: isn't it awful to know voices, instantly and certainly, by their shouts to the waggoner five floors down . . . I wish that yours was the only voice I knew that well. I like them well enough—they are both kind, and your oldest friends, which is enough to endear them . . . But I think now—forgive me—but I think now—before it is too late . . . I think we ought not to go with them, I think we ought to remain, just you and I . . . Darling—please—Please don't do up the strap —say what you think—it's not too late— Please say quickly, I heard Banjo's feet across the hall, he'll be up in a moment . . .

(*The strap-noise, surreptitious now, starts again.*)

Please don't do it up! . . . not even slowly . . .

(Wan, affectionate, ironic.) I can hear the clothes you put on in the morning . . . Your serge today, hear it and smell it—with a cornflower out of the vase: I caught that the minute you put it in your buttonhole—do you sometimes wonder whether I'm a witch . . . ? I'm only your good fairy, if you let me, and I want to stay here with you. I'll be all right, after all this time, I'm confident now, I won't be frightened, ever, even when you leave me here—and of course you will be going out—often—to visit Mouse and Banjo in their new studio—Please *say*.

BEAUCHAMP: Sophie . . . How can I say . . . ?

(Door. YOUNG MARTELLO.)

MARTELLO: Hello . . . So—what news?

BEAUCHAMP: None.

(Violently pulls strap tight.)

I'll take this down. How's the waggon?

MARTELLO: All right, but I fear for the horse—bow-backed and spindle-shanked.

BEAUCHAMP: I'll . . . come back.

(Door.)

SOPHIE: I'm sorry not to be helping. I have to sit by the window and be look-out.

MARTELLO *(laughs openly):* Oh, that's frightfully good. Always making such good fun of yourself, Sophie . . .

(Accordion.)

SOPHIE: Perhaps there will be another accordionist waiting for us across the river. And no doubt the smell will be much the same on the left bank. But I shall like the Chelsea side much better.

MARTELLO: It's a better class of people, of course. Even the artists are desperately middle-class.

SOPHIE: I was thinking of the sunshine—we'll be facing south on that bank, and we'll get the sun through our front windows. I shall sit at my new post, with the sun on my face, and imagine the view as Turner painted it. It probably has not changed so very much, apart from the colours. Don't you wish you could paint like Turner?—no, I'm sorry, of course you don't, how stupid of me . . . Well, I don't suppose Turner would have wished to paint like you. He *could* have done, of course.

MARTELLO: Of course.

SOPHIE: But he would not have wished to.

MARTELLO: It would not have occurred to him to do so; I think that's really the point.

SOPHIE: Yes, I think it really is. What are you doing now?

MARTELLO: I'm not painting now. I'm making a figure.

SOPHIE: I really meant *now*—at this moment— what are you doing here?

MARTELLO: Oh. Well, I'm not actually doing anything now, just talking to you.

SOPHIE: Can you see a hamper anywhere?

MARTELLO: A hamper? —no.

SOPHIE: There ought to be one; for my shoes and handbags.

MARTELLO: Well, wait till Biscuit comes up—I think I can hear him on the stairs.

SOPHIE: No, that's Mouse. What silly schoolboy names. When will you stop using them?

MARTELLO: I suppose they are silly when you hear them—but we never hear them because they are merely our names . . . I expect we shall stop using them when we are very old and painting like Landseer.

SOPHIE: Not without lessons. I didn't mean to sound scornful, about your names. I'm nervous about moving.

MARTELLO: Yes. Of course.

SOPHIE: Nicknames are really very touching. Did you ever play the banjo?

MARTELLO: No. I was thought to be similarly shaped when young. Biscuit kept saying, 'Well, that takes the biscuit.'

41

SOPHIE: Yes, I know. And 'Mouse' because he enters quietly.

DONNER: Hello, Sophie.

(Pause.)

SOPHIE: What *is* going on? *(Pause.)* He told me about your figure.

MARTELLO: Did he?

SOPHIE: Only that you were doing one. What is it?

MARTELLO: Well, actually it's called 'The Cripple'. It's going to be a wooden man with a real leg.

SOPHIE: A sort of joke.

MARTELLO: Yes.

SOPHIE: And will you actually use a real leg?

MARTELLO: Well, no, of course not. I shall have to make it.

SOPHIE: What will you make it of?

MARTELLO: Well, wood . . . of course.

(Pause.)

SOPHIE: How about a black-patch-man with a real eye——

MARTELLO: Sophie——

SOPHIE *(breaks—bursts out):* He doesn't know what to do with me, does he?—Well, what's going to happen?—you're all *going,* aren't you?

MARTELLO *(quietly):* Mouse is going to stay. Excuse me . . .

(Leaves, closes door.)
(Pause.)

SOPHIE *(recovered):* You're staying?

DONNER: Yes.

SOPHIE: Why?

DONNER: Either way it's what I want to do.

SOPHIE: Either way?

DONNER: If you're going with them, I don't want to live so close to you any more.

SOPHIE: If I'm going . . . ?

DONNER: Sophie, you know I love you . . . how long I've loved you . . .

SOPHIE: He wants me to stay? With you?

DONNER (cries out): Why do you want to go? (quietly) He's stopped caring for you. He only hurts you now, and I can't bear it. When he made you happy I couldn't bear it, and now that he hurts you I . . . just can't bear it——

SOPHIE: Does he love someone else?

DONNER: He hasn't got anyone else.

SOPHIE: That isn't what I asked. Does he love that poet?—that educated Bohemian with the private income?—He read me her poems, and then he stopped reading me her poems. I thought he must be seeing her.

DONNER: Only in company. I'm sure she doesn't think twice about him——

SOPHIE: Is she going with him——?

DONNER: No—of course not! . . . It's not even a suitable place to share like that—it's just one large attic room, the beds all together and just cooking gear in the corner——

SOPHIE: He never intended that I should go.

DONNER: It really is most unsuitable. The bathroom is on the landing below, with steep unprotected stairs—you could fall—Sophie, you *must* stay here, you know it here—and I'll abide by any terms——

SOPHIE: When was he going to tell me?

DONNER: Every day.

SOPHIE: Perhaps he was going to leave a note on the mantelpiece. As a sort of joke.

DONNER: Sophie . . . I love you. I'll look after you.

SOPHIE: Yes, I know you would. But I can't love you back, Mouse. I'm sorry, but I can't. I have lost the capability of falling in love. The last image that I have of love is him larking about in that gallery where you had

45

your first exhibition. 'Frontiers in Art'—what a lark you were, you three, with your paintings of barbed wire fences and signboards saying 'You are now entering Patagonia'—you were such cards, weren't you?, all of you merry, not at all like artists but like three strapping schoolboy cricketers growing your first pale moustaches. I liked you all very much. I like the way you roared with laughter at all your friends. I never heard anything any of you said, and you didn't take any notice of me at the back in my stiff frock and ribbons and my awful thick glasses, but I liked you all anyway, and bit by bit I couldn't stop looking at him, and thinking, which one is he?—Martello? Beauchamp? Donner? . . . It was quick: one moment the sick apprehension of something irrevocable which I had not chosen, and then he was the secret in the deep centre of my life. I wouldn't have called it love myself, but it seems to be the word that people use for it.

DONNER: And when you next saw us——

SOPHIE: —I couldn't see you. But at least I no longer had to wear those glasses, and I knew I looked quite pretty . . .

DONNER: You were beautiful.

Flashback

> (MARTELLO *and* SOPHIE *are climbing stairs.*
> *Above them, behind closed doors, the sound*
> *of a ping-pong game in progress.*)

MARTELLO: Quite a climb, I'm afraid . . . Five
more steps up now, and then turn left and
that will be the top floor . . .

SOPHIE: It must be a lovely big room . . .

MARTELLO: We each have our own room, actually, but we share the drawing room—Left
—jolly good show.

SOPHIE: I hear that ping-pong is quite the fad.

MARTELLO: Is it really?—please allow me . . .

> (*Door. Ping-pong loud. The rally ends with*
> *a winning shot—denoted by the hiatus*
> *where one has been led to expect, from the*
> *rhythm, contact with the 'other' bat.*)

SOPHIE: Good shot!

MARTELLO: Gentlemen, I have the honour to present to you Miss Farthingale.

(The ping-pong resumes.)

SOPHIE *(disappointed):* Oh.

MARTELLO: My friends, as you know, are called Mr. Donner and Mr. Beauchamp. Mr. Beauchamp is to your right, Mr. Donner to your left.

(The ball hits the net: familiar sound of small diminishing bounces on the table.)

SOPHIE: Bad luck.

MARTELLO: They are not in fact playing ping-pong.

SOPHIE: Oh!

MARTELLO: That is why they are momentarily taken aback. Turn it off, Beauchamp.

(Cut ping-pong.)

SOPHIE: I'm sorry.

DONNER *(hurriedly):* How do you do?

BEAUCHAMP: How do you do?

MARTELLO: There's no point in sticking out your hands like that. Miss Farthingale is blind.

BEAUCHAMP: Really, Martello, you exceed the worst possible taste——

SOPHIE: But I am—blind as a bat, I'm afraid.

BEAUCHAMP: Oh. I'm sorry.

SOPHIE: Please don't mention it.

BEAUCHAMP: I will not, of course.

SOPHIE: Oh, mention it as much as you like. And please don't worry about saying 'you see' all the time. People do, and I don't mind a bit.

MARTELLO: Would you like to sit down, Miss Farthingale . . . Please allow me . . .

SOPHIE: Oh, thank you . . . thank you so much. That is most comfortable. I hope no one will remain standing for me.

MARTELLO: Will you take tea?

SOPHIE: I should love some tea.

DONNER: We were just waiting for the kettle to boil.

MARTELLO: Indian or Singhalese?

SOPHIE: I don't think I'd know the difference.

MARTELLO: Nobody does. That's why we only keep the one.

SOPHIE: And which one is that?

MARTELLO: I haven't the slightest idea.

DONNER: It's best Assam.

(Kettle whistles.)

SOPHIE: Is that the gramophone again?

DONNER: Excuse me.

(Kettle subsides.)

BEAUCHAMP: I have been making gramophone records of various games and pastimes.

SOPHIE: Is it for the blind?

BEAUCHAMP: Heavens, no. At least . . . the idea is you listen to the sounds with your eyes closed.

SOPHIE: It's very effective. I could have kept the score just by listening.

BEAUCHAMP: Yes!—you see—sorry!—I'm trying to liberate the visual *image* from the limitations of visual *art*. The idea is to create images—pictures—which are purely *mental* . . . I think I'm the first artist to work in this field.

SOPHIE: I should think you are, Mr. Beauchamp.

BEAUCHAMP: The one you heard was my latest —Lloyd George versus Clara Bow.

SOPHIE: Goodness!, however did you persuade them?

BEAUCHAMP: No, you see——

SOPHIE: Oh—of course! Of course I see. What a very good joke, Mr. Beauchamp.

BEAUCHAMP: Yes . . . Thank you. May I play you another?—it's very quiet.

SOPHIE: Please do.

(DONNER *with tea tray.*)

DONNER: There we are. How would you like your tea, Miss Farthingale?

MARTELLO: Perhaps *you* will do us the honour, Miss Farthingale?

DONNER: Banjo!

SOPHIE: Yes . . . Yes . . . I think so.

(*Small sounds of her hands mapping the tea tray.*)

Now.

(*Tea in first. One cup. Two. Three. Four.*)

You will all take milk?

(*'Yes please' etc. One. Two. Three. Four.*)

Mr. Donner, how many lumps?

DONNER: Two please, Miss Farthingale . . .

(*One. Two.*)

DONNER: Thank you.

SOPHIE: Mr. Beauchamp?

BEAUCHAMP: None for me, thank you.

SOPHIE: Mr. Martello?

MARTELLO: And just one for me.

(One.)

SOPHIE: There we are.

(The men's tension breaks. They applaud and laugh.)

DONNER: I say, Miss Farthingale, you're an absolutely ripping girl.

SOPHIE: How very kind of you, Mr. Donner. Please do not think me 'fast' but I was no less struck by you and your friends. I thought you all very pleasant-looking and good humoured, and there was nothing I wished more than that I should find myself having tea with you all one day.

MARTELLO: I have not in fact explained to my friends . . .

SOPHIE: Oh, forgive me. I must have puzzled you. My late uncle, who was rather progressive in such things, took me to your opening day at the Russell Gallery last year.

(Pause.)

BEAUCHAMP: Forgive my asking . . . but do you often visit the art galleries?

SOPHIE: Not now, of course, Mr. Beauchamp, but I had not yet lost all of my sight in those days. Oh dear, I'm telling everything back to front.

MARTELLO: Miss Farthingale lives at the Blind School in Prince of Wales Drive. She happened to be sitting on a bench in the public garden next to the School when I walked by. She accosted me in a most shameless manner.

SOPHIE: Absolutely untrue!

MARTELLO: I have been twice to tea at the School since then. She always pours.

SOPHIE: I was in the park with my teacher, but she had left me for a few moments while she went down to the water to feed the ducks.

When she looked back she saw a gentleman with a fixed grin and a raised hat staring at me in a most perplexed and embarrassed manner. By the time she returned to rescue me, it was too late.

DONNER: Too late?

SOPHIE: I heard this voice say, 'Forgive me, but haven't we met before? My name is Martello.' Of course he'd never seen me before in his life.

MARTELLO: And she replied, 'Not the artist, by any chance?'

SOPHIE: 'I believe so,' he said, flattered I think.

MARTELLO: 'Frontiers in Art?' she asked. I was astonished. And invited to tea; with great firmness and without preamble. Now there you *were* shameless, admit it.

SOPHIE: Well, I lead such an uneventful life . . . I was naturally excited.

MARTELLO: I thought she was going to *faint* with excitement. The chaperone disapproved, even protested, but Miss Farthingale was possessed!

SOPHIE: Please, Mr. Martello . . .

BEAUCHAMP: Well, of course, the chaperone could see what you look like.

DONNER: You must have been very impressed by the exhibition, Miss Farthingale.

MARTELLO: Not by the exhibition at all! *(A bit of a faux pas, perhaps.)* I mean . . . it was Miss Farthingale's opinion that the pictures were all frivolous and not very difficult to do.

BEAUCHAMP: She was absolutely right.

MARTELLO: As I was quick to explain to her. Why should art be something difficult to do? Why shouldn't it be something very easy?

SOPHIE: But surely it is a fact about art—regardless of the artist's subject or his intentions—that it celebrates a world which includes itself—I mean, part of what there is to celebrate is the capability of the artist.

MARTELLO: How very confusing.

SOPHIE: I think every artist willy-nilly is celebrating the impulse to paint in general, the imagination to paint something in particular, and the ability to make the painting in question.

MARTELLO: Goodness!

SOPHIE: The more difficult it is to make the painting, the more there is to wonder at. It is not the only thing, but it is one of the things. And since I do not hope to impress you by tying up my own shoelace, why should you hope to have impressed me by painting a row of black stripes on a white background? Was that one of yours?

MARTELLO: I don't recall it—you asked me about it when we met.

SOPHIE: So I did. Perhaps one of your friends remembers it?—black railings on a field of snow.

MARTELLO: Let me answer for them nonetheless. You seem to forget, or perhaps you do not know, that what may seem very difficult to you may be very easy for the artist. He may paint a perfect apple as easily as you tie your shoelace, and as quickly. Furthermore, anybody could do it—yes, I insist: painting nature, one way or another, is a technique and can be learned, like playing the piano. But how can you teach someone to *think* in a certain way?—to paint an utterly simple shape in order to ambush the mind with something quite unexpected about that shape by hanging it in a frame and forcing you to see it, as it were, for the first time—

DONNER: Banjo . . .

MARTELLO: And what, after all, is the point of excellence in naturalistic art—? How does one account for, and justify, the very notion of emulating nature? The greater the success, the more false the result. It is only when the imagination is dragged away from what the eye sees that a picture becomes interesting.

SOPHIE: I think it is chiefly interesting to the artist, and to those who respond to a sense of the history of art rather than to pictures. I don't think I shall much miss what is to come, from what I know, and I am glad that I saw much of the pre-Raphaelites before my sight went completely. Perhaps you know Ruskin's essay, the one on——

BEAUCHAMP: I say, Miss Farthingale—are you wearing blue stockings?

SOPHIE: I don't know, Mr. Beauchamp. Am I? Whatever happened to the game you were going to play me?

BEAUCHAMP: Oh, it's been on. I'll turn the record over for the continuation.

DONNER: You know . . . I think I *do* remember you.

BEAUCHAMP: Now, now, Mouse.

DONNER: A girl—with spectacles, and a long pig-tail I think.

SOPHIE: Yes!

DONNER: I believe we exchanged a look!

SOPHIE: Perhaps we did. Tell me, Mr. Donner —which one were you?

DONNER: Which one?

SOPHIE: Yes. I have a picture in my mind of the three of you but I never found out, and was too shy at the time to ask, which was Donner, and which Beauchamp, and which Martello. I asked my uncle afterwards, but although he knew which of you was which, I

59

was unable to describe you with enough individuality . . .

DONNER: Shame, Miss Farthingale!

SOPHIE: Well, you were all fair, and well built. None of you had a beard or jug ears—and if you remember you were all wearing your army uniforms, all identical . . .

MARTELLO: Yes, it was a sort of joke. We had not been long back from France.

BEAUCHAMP: Late going, late returning.

SOPHIE: A few months later my blindness descended on me, and the result is that I do not know which of your voices goes with the face that has stayed in my mind—that is, all three faces, of course.

(Pause.)

BEAUCHAMP: Is it that you remember one of our faces particularly, Miss Farthingale?

SOPHIE: Well, yes, Mr. Beauchamp.

BEAUCHAMP: Oh.

SOPHIE: I mean, I thought you were all engaging.

BEAUCHAMP: But one of us more engaging than the others.

MARTELLO: Ah. Well, we shall never know!

DONNER: Oh!, but it was my eye you caught.

SOPHIE: As a matter of fact, there is a way of . . . satisfying my curiosity. There was a photographer there, for one of the illustrated magazines . . .

DONNER: The *Tatler.*

SOPHIE: No, there was no photograph in the *Tatler,* I happened to see . . . but this man posed each of you against a picture you had painted.

MARTELLO: I see. And you want to know which of us was the one who posed against the painting you have described.

SOPHIE: Well, yes. It would satisfy my curiosity. It was a background of snow, I think.

DONNER: Yes, there was a snow scene. Only one.

SOPHIE: A field of snow, occupying the whole canvas——

MARTELLO: Not the whole canvas——

SOPHIE: No—there was a railing——

BEAUCHAMP: Yes, that's it—a border fence in the snow!

SOPHIE: Yes! *(Pause.)* Well, which of you . . . ?

DONNER: It was Beauchamp you had in mind.

SOPHIE: Mr. Beauchamp!

BEAUCHAMP: Yes, Miss Farthingale . . . It seems it was me.

(Pause.)

SOPHIE *(brightly):* Well, is anybody ready for some more tea?

MARTELLO: I will replenish the pot.

(Pause.)

Harold Gould as BEAUCHAMP, the tonal artist:
Fascinating, isn't it? Layer upon layer of what passes for silence, trapped from an empty room—no, trawled. I know that in this loop of tape there is some truth about how we live. These unheard sounds which are our silence stand as a metaphor—a correspondence between the limits of hearing and the limits of all knowledge: and whose silence is our hubbub?
Photo Credit: Shel Secunda

John McMartin as DONNER, the painter:
I'm sorry, Beauchamp, but you must come to terms with the fact that our paths have diverged. I very much enjoyed my years in that child's garden of easy virtues known as the avant garde, but I am now engaged in the infinitely more difficult task of painting what the eye sees.
Photo Credit: Shel Secunda

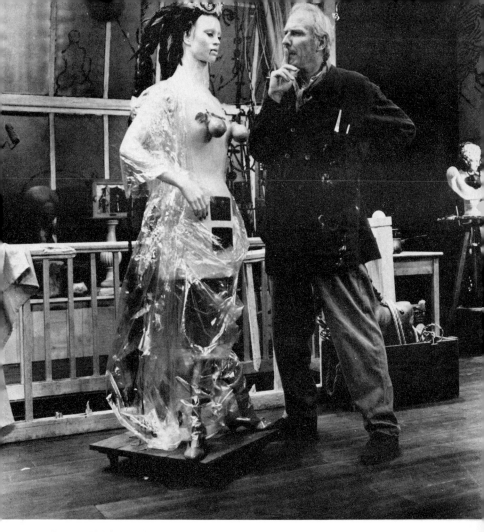

Paxton Whitehead as MARTELLO, the sculptor: How do you like her?
DONNER: It looks like a scarecrow trying to be a tailor's dummy.
 Is it symbolic?
MARTELLO: Metaphorical. . . . I don't know how to do her eyes: stars
 seem somehow inappropriate. . . . Would you have described them as
 dark pools, perhaps?
DONNER: Who?
MARTELLO: Well, Sophie, of course.
DONNER: Are you telling me that *thing* is supposed to be Sophie?
MARTELLO: Metaphorically. . . .
DONNER: You unspeakable rotter! Is nothing sacred to you?
Photo Credit: Shel Secunda

Stephanie Roth as SOPHIE, the inspiration:
Surely it is a fact about art—regardless of the artist's subject or his
intentions—that it celebrates a world which includes itself—I mean, part
of what there is to celebrate is the capability of the artist. . . . I think
every artist willy-nilly is celebrating the impulse to paint in general, the
imagination to paint something in particular, and the ability to make the
painting in question.
With Miss Roth: at left, Michael Winther; center, Michael Cumpsty and
right, Jim Fyfe.
Photo Credit: Shel Secunda

(GRAMOPHONE: *'Check.'*)

SOPHIE: Oh!—is it chess, Mr. Beauchamp?

BEAUCHAMP: It is. Lenin versus Jack Dempsey.

SOPHIE: Oh, that's very good. But do you no longer paint?

BEAUCHAMP: No. Nobody will be painting in fifty years. Except Donner, of course.

SOPHIE: Well, I hope you will paint beauty, Mr. Donner, and the subtlest beauty is in nature.

BEAUCHAMP: Oh, please don't think that I am against beauty, or nature, Miss Farthingale. Indeed, I especially enjoy the garden where you met Martello, a most delightful prospect across the river, isn't it?—I mean——

SOPHIE: You are quite right, Mr. Beauchamp. It is a delightful prospect, for me too. It is only my sight I have lost. I enjoy the view just as much as anyone who sits there with eyes closed in the sun; more, I think, because I can improve on reality, like a painter, but without fear of contradiction. Indeed, if I hear hoofbeats, I can put a unicorn in the

63

garden and no one can open my eyes against it and say it isn't true.

MARTELLO *(returning):* To the Incas, who had never seen a horse, unicorns had the same reality as horses, which is a very high degree of reality.—Listen! Miss Farthingale, is that a hansom or a landau?

(Carriage in the street below.)

SOPHIE: Eight hooves, Mr. Martello, but it's not a landau for all that. Those are shire horses, probably a brewer's dray.

MARTELLO *(at window):* A brewer's dray as I live!—More games!

BEAUCHAMP: I say—that has suddenly brought to mind—do you remember——?

MARTELLO: Yes—I was just thinking the same thing——

BEAUCHAMP: Beauchamp's Tenth Horse!

Flashback

(Clip-clop . . . BEAUCHAMP's Horse. Flies buzzing in the heat. Feet walking.)

64

BEAUCHAMP *(declaiming)*: Art consists of constant surprise. Art should never conform. Art should break its promises. Art is nothing to do with expertise: doing something well is no excuse for doing the expected. My God, this is fun. All my life I have wanted to ride through the French countryside in summer, with my two best friends, and make indefensible statements about art. I am most obliged to you, Martello. I am delighted to know you, Donner. How do you like my horse?

MARTELLO: Beautiful, your Majesty.

DONNER: Very nice. Why don't you give it a rest?

BEAUCHAMP: Mouse is a bit mousey today. You should have invested in a horse. It makes an enormous difference. In fact I have never felt so carefree. When we are old and doddery and famous and life is given over to retrospection and retrospectives, this is as far back as I want memory to go——

(Smack!)

I've never been so hot . . . and the flies . . .

(Smack!)

Are we nearly there?

MARTELLO: Nearly where?

DONNER: How do I know?

BEAUCHAMP: Secondly!—how can the artist justify himself in the community? What is his role? What is his reason?—Donner, why are you trying to be an artist?

DONNER: I heard there were opportunities to meet naked women.

BEAUCHAMP: Donner is feeling cynical.

DONNER: I had never seen a naked woman, and the way things were going I was never likely to. My family owned land.

BEAUCHAMP: Interesting line of thought; don't pretend to follow it myself. I repeat—how can the artist justify himself? The answer is that he cannot, and should stop boring people with his egocentric need to try. The artist is a lucky dog. That is all there is to say about him. In any community of a thousand souls there will be nine hundred doing the work, ninety doing well, nine doing good, and one lucky dog painting or writing about the other nine hundred and ninety-nine. Whoa, boy, whoa . . .

DONNER: Oh, shut up.

BEAUCHAMP: I don't know what to call him.

MARTELLO: I've had the most marvellous idea.

DONNER: So have I.

MARTELLO: A portrait . . . an idealization of female beauty, based on the Song of Solomon.

BEAUCHAMP: I don't get it.

DONNER: *My* idea is that next year we should go on a motoring tour, and if we can't afford a car we should stay at home.

MARTELLO: You were dead keen about a walking tour, Mouse.

DONNER: Well, I like some parts more than others. The part I liked best was the first part when we planned our route, sitting by the fire at home with a cup of cocoa and a map of France. If you remember, we decided to make the journey in easy stages, between one charming village and the next . . . setting off each morning after a simple breakfast on a terrace overhung with vines, striking out cross-country along picturesque footpaths, occasionally fording a laughing brook, resting at midday in the shade, a picnic, perhaps a nap, and then another little walk to a convenient inn . . . a hot bath, a good dinner, a pipe in the tap-room with the honest locals, and so to bed with a candle and a good book, to sleep dreamlessly——

(Smack!)

take *that* you little devil!

BEAUCHAMP *(hooves skittering):* Whoa—whoa —Try not to startle my mount, Donner.

DONNER: Oh, shut up, Biscuit. I'm bitten all day by French flies and at night the mosquitoes take over. I nearly drowned trying to cross a laughing torrent, the honest locals have stolen most of our money so that we have had to sleep rough for three days, I've had nothing to eat today except for half a coco-

nut, and as for the picturesque footpaths—
oh God, here they bloody come again!

*(Improbably, a convoy of rattletrap lorries
roars past. Between their approach and
their decline, nothing else is audible. At the
end of it,* BEAUCHAMP's *horse is skittering
about.)*

BEAUCHAMP: Steady, steady . . . good boy . . .

MARTELLO: Tell you what—give Mouse a go on
the horse.

BEAUCHAMP: No. This horse only believes in
me. What an animal!—I've had nine horses
at various times counting my first pony, but
none has been remotely like this one . . .
Absolutely no trouble, and he gives me a
magical feeling of confidence. My spirits lift,
the road slips by . . . What shall I call him?

DONNER: Where are we, Banjo? Do you know?

MARTELLO: More or less.

DONNER: Well?

MARTELLO: There's a discrepancy between the
map and the last signpost.

DONNER: There hasn't been a signpost since this morning. Perhaps they're uprooting them.

(More lorries.)

BEAUCHAMP: Steady, steady . . .

DONNER: For God's sake, Beauchamp, will you get rid of that coconut!

BEAUCHAMP: Coconut!—not a bad name. And yet it lacks a certain something. Would Napoleon have called his horse Coconut? . . . Napoleon . . . not a bad name.

DONNER: Apart from anything else, it's becoming increasingly clear that we should have stayed at home because of the international situation.

MARTELLO: What international situation?

DONNER: The war.

MARTELLO: What war? You don't believe any of that rot. Why should there be a war? Those Middle Europeans are always assassinating each other.

DONNER: That's the fourth lot of troop lorries we've met today, and we haven't seen a newspaper all week.

MARTELLO: The French are an excitable people.

DONNER: But they weren't French, they were German.

MARTELLO: Rubbish.

DONNER: Yes they were.

MARTELLO: Where's that bloody map? Biscuit, were those lorries French or German?

BEAUCHAMP: I don't know, Banjo. One lorry is much like another.

MARTELLO: I mean the soldiers. Donner says they were German.

BEAUCHAMP: How does one tell?

MARTELLO: Well, Donner?

DONNER: The uniforms.

MARTELLO: The uniforms. Well, don't worry. They're going in the opposite direction. By the time they get to Paris we'll be in Switzerland.

DONNER: Do you seriously expect me to walk to Switzerland? You're crazy, Martello.

(Dull distant explosion; field gun.)

MARTELLO: Quarrying.

BEAUCHAMP: All right, Napoleon, easy, boy . . .

DONNER: Beauchamp's crazy too.

(Explosion, repeat.)

BEAUCHAMP: I know!—I'll call him Beauchamp's Tenth Horse!—He will be the phantom cavalry that turns the war—now you see him, now you don't—he strikes, and is gone, his neigh lost on the wind, he leaves no hoofprints; there is only the sound of his hooves on the empty road—He's not physical!—He's not metaphysical!—He's pataphysical!—apocalyptic, clipcloptic, Beauchamp's Tenth!—Here it comes—!!

(A squadron of Cavalry gallops in quickly to occupy the foreground with a thunder of hooves; and recedes, leaving the men stunned and sobered.)

MARTELLO: Good Christ.

DONNER: Now do you believe me? They were German cavalry.

BEAUCHAMP: He's right.

MARTELLO: We must have got too far east. Don't worry—good God, if a man can't go for a walk on the Continent nowadays, what is the world coming to? Come on; I see there's a fork in the road—judging by the sun the right fork is the Swiss one.

(Explosion.)

Take no notice.

DONNER: Look what's that?

MARTELLO: What?—Ah. Men digging a ditch.

BEAUCHAMP: Soldiers.

MARTELLO: It is not unusual for soldiers to do such work in France. Or Germany. The main thing is to ignore them.

BEAUCHAMP: That's quite a ditch.

MARTELLO: Isn't it? Laying pipes, I shouldn't wonder.

BEAUCHAMP: Would you call that a trench?

MARTELLO: Take no notice.

DONNER: We'll probably be interned. I hope they'll do it with some kind of transport.

MARTELLO: Beautiful bit of country, this. The road is climbing. That's a good sign. Come on, Biscuit. What happened to your Tenth Horse?

BEAUCHAMP: My feet are swelling visibly— Good lord!

(A shock.)

MARTELLO *(talking up and out):* Good morning!

BEAUCHAMP *(ditto):* Bonjour!

74

DONNER: Gut'n tag . . .

(Pause).

BEAUCHAMP *(whisper):* That was a field gun!

MARTELLO: My dear chap, it's nothing to do with us. These Continentals are always squabbling over their frontiers.

DONNER: How are we going to get back?

BEAUCHAMP: By train. I shall telegraph for money.

DONNER: There won't be any *trains!*

BEAUCHAMP: Then I shall wait at the station until there are.

DONNER: They might think we're spies . . . and kill us. That would be ridiculous. I don't want to die *ridiculously.*

BEAUCHAMP: All deaths in war are ridiculous.

MARTELLO: Now look here, you two, you're talking like tenderfeet. I am older than you; I have a little more experience. I have studied the European situation minutely, and I can assure you that there will be no war, at least not this year. You forget I have an Uncle Rupert in the War Office. I said to my uncle, when they shot that absurd Archduke Ferdinand of Ruritania, Uncle!, I said, does this mean war?—must I postpone the walking tour which I and my friends have been looking forward to since the winter?! My boy, he said—go!, go with my personal assurance. There will be no war for the very good reason that His Majesty's Government is not *ready* to go to war, and it will be six months at least before we are strong enough to beat the French.

DONNER: The French?

MARTELLO: Go and walk your socks off, my uncle said, and then take the waters-waters at Baden-Baden, to which my auntie added, perhaps that will cure you of all that artistic nonsense with which you waste your time and an expensive education. You live in a sane and beautiful world, my auntie said, and the least you can do, if you must be a painter, is to paint appropriately sane and beautiful pictures. Which reminds me—I've stopped being auntie now, by the way—I was going to tell you about my next work, a beautiful woman, as described in the Song of Solomon . . .

(Explosions build.)

I shall paint her navel as a round goblet which wanteth not liquor, her belly like a field of wheat set about with lilies, yea, her two breasts will be like two young roes that are twins, her neck as a tower of ivory, and her eyes will be like the fishpools in Hebdon by the gate of Bath-rabbim, her nose like the tower of Lebanon which looketh towards Damascus . . . Behold she will be fair! My love will have her hair as a flock of goats that appear from Mount Gilead, her teeth like a flock of sheep that are even shorn . . . I shall paint her lips like a thread of scarlet!, and her temples will be like a piece of pomegranate within her locks . . . !

(Explosions.)

End of Flashback

(The three young men are chanting out directions, sometimes in unison, sometimes just one or two voices.)

77

ALL THREE: Left! . . . left . . . right . . . left
. . . right . . . right . . . turn . . . right a bit
. . . left a bit . . . turn . . . left . . . turn
. . . stop!

DONNER: Well?

SOPHIE: I am exactly where I started, standing
with my back to my chair.

DONNER: Are you quite sure of that, Miss Farthingale?

SOPHIE *(sits):* There!

(Gasps; laughs.)

BEAUCHAMP: You win—but we might have
moved the chair.

SOPHIE: I assumed that you would move it back
if necessary, or at least catch me in your
arms.

BEAUCHAMP: Yes, you may be sure of that.

DONNER: Indeed, yes. In fact, why don't we do
it again?

SOPHIE: Not this time, Mr. Donner. I've stayed much longer than I intended, and I don't want them to worry about me at the school.

BEAUCHAMP: Then we'll walk back with you.

SOPHIE: Thank you. But there is really no need to trouble you all.

BEAUCHAMP: I should like to.

SOPHIE: Well, if you would like to, Mr. Beauchamp.

DONNER: We would all like to.

SOPHIE: Goodness, I *will* raise their eyebrows—oh!!

(She has knocked over the tea-table.)

BEAUCHAMP: Martello!—you moved the tea things!

SOPHIE: I'm so sorry—how clumsy——

BEAUCHAMP: It wasn't your fault one bit—please get up—really—There!—oh——

SOPHIE: What is it?

BEAUCHAMP: Only that you *are* wearing blue stockings!

(SOPHIE *and* BEAUCHAMP *laugh.*)

MARTELLO: You seem to be in very good hands, Miss Farthingale. I'm sure you don't want to be accompanied by a whole gang of people, so permit me to say good-bye, and I hope that you will come again.

SOPHIE: Oh, Mr. Martello—of course. Thank you so much again. And good-bye to you both.

DONNER: Oh . . . Good-bye, Miss Farthingale.

MARTELLO: I hope Mr. Beauchamp will not leave you without inviting you to dinner.

BEAUCHAMP: Wouldn't dream of it.

SOPHIE: I should love to come to dinner. Oh— and there will be no need to dress . . . Come then, Mr. Beauchamp . . . may I hold your hand on the stairs?

BEAUCHAMP: If we are going to hold hands, I think I ought to know your name.

SOPHIE: It's Sophie.

DONNER: Don't fall . . .

BEAUCHAMP: I won't!

(Their laughter receding down the stairs.)

DONNER *(close, quiet):* Don't fall.

(Door closes on the laughter.)

End of Flashback

(Faint accordion as before. Feet descending the stairs, starting outside the closed door of the room, and getting fainter with each succeeding floor. They are still faintly audible at the very bottom, and the last sound, just audible, is the front door slamming. This whole business probably takes half a minute. After the slam, SOPHIE speaks close up.)

SOPHIE: I feel blind again. I feel more blind than I did the first day, when I came to tea. I shall blunder about, knocking over the occasional table.
(Cries out.) It's not possible!—What is he thinking of?—What are *you* thinking of,

Mouse? . . . We can't live here like brother and sister. I know you won't make demands of me, so how can I make demands of you? Am I to weave you endless tablemats and antimacassars in return for life? . . . And is the servant girl to be kept on? I cannot pay her and I cannot allow you to pay her in return for the privilege of reading to me in the evenings. And yet I will not want to be alone, I cannot live alone, I am afraid of the dark; not *my* dark, the real dark, and I need to know that it's morning when I wake or I will fear the worst and never believe in the dawn breaking—who will do that for me? . . . And who will light the fire; and choose my clothes so the colours don't clash; and find my other shoe; and do up my dress at the back? You haven't thought about it. And if you have then you must think that I will be your lover. But I will not. I cannot. And I cannot live with you knowing that you want me—Do you see that? . . . Mouse? Are you here? Say something. Now, don't do that, Mouse, it's not fair—please, you are here . . . Did you go out? Now please don't . . . How can I do anything if I can't trust you—I beg you, if you're here, tell me. What do you want? Are you just going to watch me?— standing quietly in the room—sitting on the bed—on the edge of the tub—Watch me move about the room, grieving, talking to myself, sleeping, washing, dressing, undressing, crying?—Oh no, there is no way now—I won't—I won't—I won't—no, I won't . . . !

(Glass panes and wood smash violently. Silence. In the silence, hoofbeats in the street, then her body hitting, a horse neighing.)

End of Flashback

MARTELLO: She would have killed you, Donner. I mean if she'd fallen a yard to the right. Brained you or broken your back, as you waved us good-bye. I remember I heard the glass go and looked up, but my mind seized and I shouted 'Look out' after she hit. I wouldn't have saved you. Beauchamp said she fell, an accident; otherwise why didn't she open the window, he said. I don't know, though. Why should she have behaved rationally to fulfil an irrational impulse? 'This tragic defenestration,' the coroner said. I remember that. Pompous fool, I thought. But I suppose he looked on it as a rare chance to use the word. It's an odd word to exist, defenestration, isn't it? I mean when you consider the comparatively few people who have jumped or been thrown from windows to account for it. By the way, I'm still missing one of her teeth, can you see it anywhere?—a pearl, it could have rolled under the cupboard . . . Yes, why isn't there a word, in that case, for people being pushed downstairs or stuffed up chimneys . . . ? De-escalate is a word, I believe, but they don't use it for that. And, of course, influence. He was bodily in-fluenced. That's a good idea; let's cheer ourselves up by inventing verbs for various kinds of fatality——

DONNER: Martello, will you please stop it.

(Pause.)

MARTELLO: Oh, there it is.

DONNER: Her teeth were broken too, smashed, scattered . . .

MARTELLO: *Donner!* If there is anything to be said it's not that. Fifty years ago we knew a nice girl who was due for a sad life, and she jumped out of a window, which was a great shock and certainly tragic, and here we are, having seen much pain and many deaths, none of them happy, and no doubt due for our own one way or another, and then we will have caught up on Sophie's fall, all much of a muchness after a brief delay between the fall of one body and another——

DONNER: No, no, each one is vital and every moment counts—what other reason is there for trying to work well and live well and choose well? I think it was a good life lost— she would have been happy with me.

MARTELLO: Well, Beauchamp thought the same, but they were only happy for a year or two. How can you tell? A blind mistress is a difficult proposition.

DONNER: I would have married her without question.

MARTELLO: Well, yes, perhaps one made the wrong choice.

DONNER: There was no choice. She fell in love with him at first sight. As I did with her, I think. After that, even when life was at its best there was a small part missing and I knew that I was going to die without ever feeling that my life was complete.

MARTELLO: Is it still important, Donner? Would it comfort you if you thought, even now, that Sophie loved you?

DONNER: I can never think that, but I wish I could be sure that she had some similar feeling for me.

MARTELLO: Did you ever wonder whether it was you she loved?

DONNER: No, of course not. It was Beauchamp.

MARTELLO: To *us* it was Beauchamp, but which of us did she see in her mind's eye . . . ?

DONNER: But it *was* Beauchamp—she remembered his painting, the snow scene.

MARTELLO: Yes. She asked me whether I had painted it within five minutes of meeting me in the garden that day; she described it briefly, and I had an image of black vertical railings, like park railings, right across the canvas, as though one were looking at a field of snow through the bars of a cage; not like Beauchamp's snow scene at all.

DONNER: But it was the only snow scene.

MARTELLO: Yes, it was, but—I promise you, Donner, it was a long time afterwards when this occurred to me, when she was already living with Beauchamp——

DONNER: What occurred to you, Martello?

MARTELLO: Well, your painting of the white fence——

DONNER: White fence?

MARTELLO: Thick white posts, top to bottom across the whole canvas, an inch or two apart, black in the gaps——

DONNER: Yes, I remember it. Oh God.

MARTELLO: Like looking at the dark through the gaps in a white fence.

DONNER: Oh my God.

MARTELLO: Well, one might be wrong, but her sight was not good even then.

DONNER: Oh my God.

MARTELLO: When one thinks of the brief happiness she enjoyed . . . well, we thought she was enjoying it with Beauchamp but she was really enjoying it with you. As it were.

DONNER: Oh my God.

MARTELLO: Of course, it was impossible to say so, after she got off on the right foot with Beauchamp—I mean, one couldn't——

DONNER: Oh my God!

MARTELLO: Now, steady on, Donner, or I'll be sorry I mentioned it——

DONNER: *Oh my God* . . .

End of Flashback

(Smack!)

BEAUCHAMP: Missed him again! *(Pause.)* All right, don't tell me then.

(BEAUCHAMP*'s* TAPE: *snap crackle pop . . .)*

Fascinating, isn't it? Layer upon layer of what passes for silence, trapped from an empty room—no, trawled—no, like—no matter: I know that in this loop of tape there is some truth about how we live, Donner. These unheard sounds which are our silence stand as a metaphor—a correspondence between the limits of hearing and the limits of all knowledge: and whose silence is our hubbub?

DONNER: Are you going out, Beauchamp? I'd like to get on.

BEAUCHAMP: I have nothing to go out for.

DONNER: Get some fly-killer.

BEAUCHAMP: All right, if you'll let me record a clean loop while I'm out. I don't want you whistling, and throwing things about when you can't get the likeness right.

DONNER: I *am* getting it right.

BEAUCHAMP: Yes, she's very good. May I make a small suggestion?

DONNER: No.

BEAUCHAMP: Her nipples were in fact——

DONNER: Get out!

BEAUCHAMP: Courtesy costs nothing. All right, I'll see if Martello is in the pub, and I'll be back in an hour or so.

(Changing tapes.)

There. Will you press the switch when I'm out of the door?

DONNER: Yes.

BEAUCHAMP: Promise?

DONNER: I promise, Beauchamp.

BEAUCHAMP: Poor Sophie. I think you've got her, Donner.

(BEAUCHAMP'*s feet down the stairs. Open and close door. The fly starts to buzz. It comes close to the microphone and the sound is distorted slightly into a droning rhythm.)*

End of Flashback

(The beginning of the DONNER TAPE. *It is the same sound as made by the fly.)*

MARTELLO: I don't want to hear it again.

(Cut TAPE.*)*

BEAUCHAMP: Now then. Let's try looking at it backwards. Coolly. Fact number one: Donner is lying at the bottom of the stairs, dead, with what looks to my untrained eye like a broken neck. Inference: he fell down the stairs. Fact number two: the balustrade up here is broken. Inference: Donner fell through it, as a result of, er, staggering and possibly slipping on what is undeniably a slippery floor, as a result of . . . Well, fact number three: the sounds which correspond to these inferences were preceded by Donner crying out, preceded by a sort of thump, preceded by two quick footsteps, preceded by Donner remarking, unalarmed—I can't believe it of you, Martello!

(Pause.)

MARTELLO: Nor I of you, Beauchamp. *(Pause.)* Well, let's get him upstairs.

BEAUCHAMP: Hang on . . .

(Fly.)

That fly has been driving me mad. Where is he?

MARTELLO: Somewhere over there . . .

BEAUCHAMP: Right.

The original loop of TAPE *is hereby reproduced:*
   (a) Fly droning.
   *(b) Careful footsteps approach. A
         board creaks.*
   (c) The fly settles.
   (d) BEAUCHAMP halts.
   (e) BEAUCHAMP: 'Ah! There you are.'
   *(f) Two more quick steps and then:
         Thump!*

BEAUCHAMP: Got him!

(Laughs shortly.)

'As flies to wanton boys are we to the
   Gods:
they kill us for their sport.'
Now then.